DATE DUE

In Medias Res

♦

In Medias Res

A PRIMER OF EXPERIENCE
IN APPROXIMATE
ALPHABETICAL
ORDER

Karen An-hwei Lee

Winner of the 2003
Kathryn A. Morton Prize in Poetry
Selected by Heather McHugh

Sarabande Books
LOUISVILLE, KENTUCKY

No part of this book may be reproduced without written permission of
the publisher. Please direct inquiries to:

Managing Editor
Sarabande Books, Inc.
2234 Dundee Road, Suite 200
Louisville, KY 40205

Library of Congress Cataloging-in-Publication Data

Lee, Karen An-hwei, 1973–
In medias res : poems / by Karen An-hwei Lee.— 1st ed.
p. cm.
"Winner of the 2003 Kathryn A. Morton Prize in Poetry."
ISBN 1-932511-06-7 (acid-free paper) — ISBN 1-932511-07-5
(pbk. : acid-free paper)
I. Title.
PS3612.E3435 I5 2004
811'.6—dc22   2003024435

Cover image: "Intercessory Prayer" by Cornelis Monsma. Oil on can-
vas, 100 x 120 cm, 39 x 47 inches. Provided courtesy of the artist.
www.monsmart.com

Cover and text design by Charles Casey Martin

Manufactured in Canada
This book is printed on acid-free paper.

Sarabande Books is a nonprofit literary organization.

Special thanks to the following most generous supporters: Anonymous
(2), John and Penny Barr, Matthew and Brooke Barzun, Stephen Reily
and Emily Bingham, Edward and Nina Bonnie, Kurt Brown and Laure
Anne Bosselaar, Christy and Owsley Brown II, Linda Bruckheimer, Sue
Driskell, Dick and Jeanne Fisher, Sandra Anne Frazier, Lisa Brown
and Daniel Handler, John Jacob, May Weatherby Jones, Joe and
Joanne Oldham, Susan Griffin and Douglas Sharps, Alice and J.
Walker Stites, Kate Walbert, James and Marianne Welch.

FIRST EDITION

for SANDRA ANN JONES

whose eyes are healed
in the midst of things

Contents

♦

Introduction

✦

Karen Lee's *In Media∫ Re∫* is an étude on blindness and enlightenment. It distinguishes itself from many other wonderful books by bringing to conservative spiritual resources a taste for radical structural innovation. I can't remember ever before having seen a poet go after Christian insight with the lenses and frames of a Gertrude Stein; had you asked me (before I had read *In Media∫ Re∫*) I would have judged such an enterprise unlikely to turn out well for poetry. But lo and behold! This is a very bright book.

Its taxonomic daring is vintage Stein: the work is divided into alphabetized subunits with a range of mysterious titles (CELL, CHATOYANCY, CLICKING SOUNDS, CONUNDRUM, CASEMENT, for example; or EMBARCADERO, EMBER DAYS, EDGE OF FAITH, EXPLODING THE BOX; or GRASS FLOWERS, GERMINATION, GIRANDOLE, GLASS WITHIN GLASS, GOLDEN-SHOD FEET, GRAND THEFT). Most sections contain only a few lines (INHERITANCE reads "A light bulb, filament unharmed, birds of glass, and a thimble."). There are collage effects: Many snippets contain quotations from popular sources such as the *Life Science Library*, the *Ladies' Home Journal Book of Interior Decoration*, the *Book of Knowledge* and the publications of various evangelical ministries.

That such material can be charged and changed by Lee's strange and gemological arrangements is the measure of her gift: the book as a whole seeks to find words for a woman's loss of her sight, and the human capacity to make sense of the patterns and accidents of life. Her theology sometimes seems a sort of rheology, for the figures of sight, which at some points take on the hard transparency of precious stones, can at other times appear as fluid as water: and indeed the book as a whole is a streaming itemization, full of bobbing objects in a sensory flow. Where others might find "blind fortune," Lee finds "unseen wealth." Among entries under the letter I the following telling instance appears:

AN INNING OR AN EAR

Passing through one's mind without making an impression.
A space in the upper corner of a weather forecast.
A line used to fasten a corner of a sail to the yard.
Land reclaimed from the sea.
The day and hour unknown.

[X]

Fenestrae in the ear.

A sympathetic attention.

That attention is a form of prayer is a mystic's intuition. But Lee also has Stein's gift for logophiliacal inquiry and measured skepticism. And like Moore, she relishes peculiar facts—e.g., that "ear stones" are a metaphor of blindness; or that there are fenestrae (windows) in the ear. Such facts are the facets of her offering: they glitter against the gem-box's black lining. Best of all, Lee has a fine paronomastic flair. She highlights but does not belabor the affinities between words—box and books, grasses and glasses, cell and shell. (A cell is as surely a feature of a prison as of the structure of biological life; a shell is as surely the casing for a charge of gunpowder as it is an impersonal manner concealing emotion, a thin layer of stone, or a narrow light racing boat: such paradoxes are Lee's signature and lexicographical delight. Like Stein, she reminds us that literary content has most of all to do with the uncontainable.)

For Lee, the apperceptive faculty is a spiritual one, and it makes waves in our measures of space and time. Obscurity can reveal and glasses can burn. These facts turn, under her steady gaze, into insights. Lee's sense of things' senses is subtly evocative, richly figured.

[XI]

Perhaps the best recommendation to readers, in the end, is formed of Lee's own words. From under the letter L, I quote the following snippet in its entirety. Its title alone suggests plenty about the book's wit and wherewithal, its sphere of stirring influence:

LIMITED OMNISCIENCE

The eye flaring.

One's eye healed.

A minute past the hour.

A parcel of rain.

A water marble.

A spirit of sight.

— Heather McHugh

Zoe received in sufficient measure
transforms us *from glory to glory*
into the image of Christ.
> —*Christ the Healer* by F. F. Bosworth

In Medias Res

♦

- A -

ACAJOU

West Indian tree varying from flesh to auburn.

Hard tropical wood of the mahogany family.

APRICOT

One morning, the day room is too much.

Too much glare from the light.

She opens a letter from her mother.

ASTERISM

A first bicycle, her father folding a paper airplane, her
mother's history books, her daughter asking, *how long
did it take you to write a hundred pages,* sapphire star hiding
inside my heart, *asterism,* the widening and questioning
look of the blind woman when I say, *it's over there; now
it's gone.*

[3]

ALTIMETER

A box of breath. The thin walls of the box are pushed in as air presses from outside. A part of the ear, I believe, behaves this way. I believe it's the *tympanum, or a drum.* It may be useful in flight.

ANTIQUE

A brandy decanter in the day room, four feet tall, amber, very still, and still very beautiful. It's in the shape of a woman, a caryatid. Standing is her vocation. Her long hair, her face, her feet, her long hands. The old couple never tasted the brandy for all the years she stood quietly corinthian in a corner of the day room.

- B -

A BASIL OR BASALT OCEAN

Sounds like slate or bay salt.

BREAKFRONT

The center is *deeper than the sides.*

Doors above and wooden doors or drawers below.

Triple bookcase or china closet.

BIRTH

The wind bloweth where it listeth. . . .

BOXES MADE OF PAPER

The eclipse is happening on paper.

Paper shelter, a sliver, scissors.

Look at the image of the sun, not directly at it.

BACHELOR CHEST

With a folding top or shelf for writing.

A BOX OF WINE

A box or bag of wine with a spigot.

BATT

Cotton for filling mattresses and for upholstering.

[5]

BREAD IN A BOX

Not cassava, the rich root used instead of flour. This mix comes out of a box. Prepare with your hands. It's rough, like cornmeal, says the blind woman. A little bit goes a long way. I'm not sure whether this flour contains ground lime. No weevils will appear in this, nor weavers who shuttle inside the bread bag.

◆ C ◆

CARATS

18 parts gold.

18-carat gold.

6 parts *other*.

14 parts gold.

14-carat gold.

10 parts *other*.

CELL

A one-room dwelling occupied by a solitary person.

A single room for one person.

A small compartment (as in a honeycomb).

A receptacle (as the calyculus of a polyp).

A bounded space (as in an insect wing).

A microscopic mass bounded by a membrane.

A receptacle (as a cup or jar).

A single unit in a device for converting radiant energy.

One-to-one correspondence with a set of points.

A basic subdivision of memory that can hold one unit
(such as a word).

CALIBRATIONS

Points on a plane, aerodynamics.

Increments of faith.

Waiting after the spoken word.

For the manifestation of miracles.

CHANGES

Winter upholstery, white to scarlet.

Or scarlet to white in winter.

CHARACTER PURPOSE

A makeshift shelter, spectrum of radiance, a city burn-
ing, vigilance, the tides arching under night skies. There
was no aimlessness to her wandering. *How long did it take
you to live a hundred pages?*

CHATOYANCY

Impurities are *lined up inside a sapphire.* The impurities,
usually rutile, produce *a pointed star. Asterism.* The pres-
ence of *needlelike impurities in parallel,* however, produces
a lustrous band of light that moves as the stone is turned. This
effect is called *chatoyancy.*

CHILDREN ASK QUESTIONS

What happens to the birds?

How does fire burn in the rain?

Does a ship have skin? Is it sweet?

[8]

How much yellow paper can we use?

We would like to write stories.

Which stones are precious minerals?

What is the *other* that is not gold?

CLICKING SOUNDS

The whispering of barnacles closing with the ebbing tide.

CONUNDRUM

Sapphires are crystals colored with traces of titanium. *Conundrums*. Rubies are also conundrums. Colored with traces of chromium. *Corundrum*, isn't it? A typographical error in the blind woman's book of knowledge. Or are sapphires and rubies true *conundrums*, mysteries harvested from underground mineral rain?

COUNTING FINGERS

Four hundreds and five ones.
Four hundred and five.
Only she remembers the ancient counting system.
She holds up her hands. *Four hundreds.*

[9]

CRUCIAL

You open the base of the bird.

The most important fold forms a diamond.

Fold over the points to form the wings.

Open the whole bird.

COMPARISON

A paper bird unopened until marriage.

CASEMENT

A window opening *on upright hinges.*

CARGO

Naval architecture, nautical words, whole ships of meaning.

DADO

Part of the wall below a chair rail.

DORMER

A window built into a sloping roof.

DETAIL AT RIGHT

This painted chair *with its one large arm.*

This room *designed for a child.*

The special arrangement of shutters inside this room.

DETAIL AT LEFT

Deep blue is eminently practical.

DIFFRACTION

One facet to another.

A child holds up his hands.

His life through slatted blinds.

He opens his eyes.

DECAY

No sound lasts forever as a sound.

[11]

DISCOVERY

Unbelievably marine.

She leaves to mourn.

What a woman's heart weighs.

A DYING MOVEMENT

It seemed she had been dreaming this for years.

Nine ounces.

Life was already enclosed.

It had casements, bachelor chests, girandoles.

ECLOSION

To emerge from a pupal case.

EIDETIC

Accurate and vivid recall of visual images.

Photographs or film of her father folding a paper plane.

Her mother, young, riding a bicycle for the first time.

Replacing the kitchen sink with her own hands.

Dropping thimbles of salt in the corners.

EAU DE VIE

Water of life . . . aqua vitae. A clear brandy distilled from the fermented juice of fruit (as pears or raspberries).

EFFERENT

Outward rather than afferent.

ELL

Addition to a house at right angles.

EMBARCADERO

A landing place on an inland waterway.

EMBER DAYS

A Wednesday, Friday, or Saturday following the first Sunday.

EDGE OF FAITH

Cut a piece of paper into a square. *Place a dime in the center of the square.* Cut out a circle with scissors. Fold the paper in half and place a quarter in the circle. *An edge of the coin will appear.* Hold the folded paper by both ends and *gently bend the edges upward.* The coin will pass through.

ETHERS AND ESTERS

Make the bouquet deep and full.

EMINENCE

I once wrote, *the sky is the color of eminence.*

ENDURANCE

Words were her paths, and she was walking on them.

EXPLODING THE BOX

Broadening light and *pillaring corners,* naming tones, *empire rose, chilled wine, burgundy,* time passing *in medias res. Of that day and hour knoweth no man, no, not the angels of heaven, but my Father only.* I would paint the walls of this room, awaiting the last hour, for my translation from flesh to spirit. *By your patience possess your souls.* I would hope for swiftness and silence, not a force that would *explode the box* containing my soul. Leaving fragments to be gathered up by God. I trust in God, however, to gather up the pieces, to grant me a healing sea of holiness, my own annealing sea.

ENTERING THESE SPACES

It is always God's will to heal.

ESCRITOIRE

She tucks the letter in her pocket.
Usually with drawers only in the apron.
A letter from her mother.

ESCUTCHEON

Ornament used over keyholes.

FALSE COVE

In a natural or false cove near the ceiling.

FIGHTING FISH

A small brilliantly colored long-finned freshwater fish.

A FINE SENSE OF BALANCE

The motion of fluid in the inner ear.

FIRST ROOM

A table.

A sacred lamp stand.

Shewbread.

FLOURLESS TORTE

The women stared through the tinted restaurant window.

The flourless torte was tall enough to be seen.

How much does it cost? The women stared.

Nine ounces, said a stranger in the dream. *Nine ounces.*

FOG

... Shuts down the sea.

FORMS OF SEEING

When I see the words *optic nerve,* I see the sea.

FUSTIAN

Once a stout cloth of cotton and flax.

GRASS FLOWERS

Their private parts are *shielded by tough paper scales.*

GERMINATION

Parsley doesn't like too much sun.

It's still folded up inside itself.

Basil requires much water.

Basil or bay salt?

Is it possible to hear seeds opening?

They harbor a gentle inward focus.

GIRANDOLE

Circular mirror....

GLASS WITHIN GLASS

A cry flowering within, refreshing and burning.

GOLDEN -SHOD FEET

A door or a box and a bird.

Changing the locks on the doors.

Anointing the doors with olive oil.

A bird flying out of the box....

A lid is like a door, says the blind woman.

A letter is like a room.

She walks quietly on golden-shod feet.

She is the blind gardener who paves the stone path.

The rows are marked by certain stones.

GRAND THEFT

I heard about a woman who stole a statue of Christ, taking Him to a hospital where she knew someone who needed Him. The statue, carved of mahogany, weighed ninety pounds. An enormous rose flourished within His soul, inside the polished auburn wood. He weighed only ninety pounds at the end of his life, perhaps, or the sculptor happened to use ninety pounds of mahogany.

HIDDEN SALT

I note the soft place on the landing, shuffle my shoes there, and would like to know whether the sea has an imagination. Salt has an imagination, replies my godchild, showing the gritty salt in his hands from the blind woman's cabinet. It imagines itself at home in the sea. Salt.

HEAVY AS DRONES

The blind woman wipes up the bread flour and corn-meal in the kitchen. I put the boxes in the cabinets. All that remains is the salt in the child's hands. Carpenter bees, heavy as drones, are gathering outside the window. They are large and slow, carving the wood under the eaves and inside the rain gutters until it looks alveolar, honeycombed for breath in the spring. The child rubs his hands, breathing quietly, and no one hears the salt dropping grain by grain.

THE HEARING OF A FLY

Nearly all insects, including the bees, ants, and wasps, are deaf.

HOUR BY HOUR

Rare birds cry in the unsheltered parts of the world.

HOW A LIGHTHOUSE IS

Each stone weighs a ton apiece.

HOW NOT TO GRIEVE THE HEART OF JESUS

The age of miracles has not yet passed.

She wiped the feet of Christ with her hair.

She poured perfume from an alabaster jar.

Mahogany is a dark and fragrant wood.

It must be polished and oiled until it yields a soft luster.

Did He weigh ninety pounds at the end of His life?

Light enough to carry, except for the burden of grief.

An unseen rose flourishes inside her mind.

He carried all the grief of the world.

HOW YOU COULD TELL SHE WAS SAD

She chose four red-skinned potatoes.

She left one bundle of spinach.

She murmured, *Celery root tastes bitter like licorice.*

[21]

-I-

IN QUARTERS

For hair money or bay leaves or cloves.

INHERITANCE

A light bulb, filament unharmed, birds of glass, and a thimble.

INNER SPACE

A space at or near the earth's surface especially under the sea. One's inner self.

INSTANT FAIENCES

At night, the blind woman hears hymning, instant faiences, gold and deep in the fundamentals, within herself. Soon, she sleeps as ships with *rutile* attentive lights flicker in silence.

AN INNING OR AN EAR

Passing through one's mind without making an impression.

A space in the upper corner of a weather forecast.

A line used to fasten a corner of a sail to the yard.

Land reclaimed from the sea.

The day and hour unknown.

Fenestrae in the ear.

A sympathetic attention.

IN THE MIDST OF THINGS

*For as the lightning cometh out of the east, and shineth even unto
the west, so shall also the coming of the Son of man be.*

-J-

JOSEPH OF ARIMATHEA

Lifts the redolent body to his tomb.

The man's surname like a crimson blossom.

Amaryllis or azalea.

JOURNEYS BY THE SEA

Sun as a flaring well of gold.

Riding bicycles with fishing poles.

Salt wrappers and laundry.

A water marble in the rain gutter.

The sand-washed street.

Bougainvillea.

A blind woman's glasses.

-K-

KINDLING POINT

Curved glass acts like a burning-glass.

KEEL

The backbone of a ship.

·L·

LIMITED OMNISCIENCE

The eye flaring.

One's eye healed.

A minute past the hour.

A parcel of rain.

A water marble.

A spirit of sight.

A LITTLE WATER EXTENDS LIFE

I learned that a little water at the bottom of the votive glass keeps the candle from sliding. I wondered whether the water would also extend its life. The candle's, that is. I wondered how much a little was, and how long the candle's wick would be in order to be useful. Whether it needed frequent trimming. How much oil.

LATE FREEZE

Each ring, *a light one and a dark one,* is half a growing season.

[25]

LAMBREQUIN

A piece of cloth *at the top of a window.*

LIVING STONES

*Some living stones grow in sand with only their windows, por-
tions of leaves where light enters, exposed at the surface. They
are impossible to find until they flower.*

LOOKS LIKE

Inside a seed or an eye.

Imperfect alphabetical order.

Tender retina.

Chatoyancy.

LOVE AT FIRST SIGHT

Solid mahogany, russeting.

-M-

MACLE

A twin crystal.

A flat, often triangular diamond.

A dark spot (as in a mineral).

MAKING THINGS STRETCH

A little rice goes a long way.

Hand soap goes a long way.

Light goes a long way on the step at night.

She goes outside to read the letter.

MARIAS

Long rills on the lunar surface.

A MEMORY

In four years, she would say, *I once was.*

Photographs are in order, the letter would say.

Without faces, yet the names are in order.

The blind woman touches the photographs.

Are they in alphabetical order?

Are these faces without names, or vice versa?

MELODRAMA

A music box dying in the ninth aisle of the dime store.

MINERALS

In all, scientists have identified more than two thousand miner-

als. Most have never been part of a living thing.

MIST

Are we in the sky yet?

My godson opens his hands, grains of salt.

MULLION

A hyphen *between panes of glass in a window.*

-N-

NAMES OF GRASS

orchard

rye

canary

reed

timothy

NAMES OF WIND

foehn

mistral

harmattan

sirocco

NEGATIVE CAPABILITY

Who speaks?

Who writes?

NEWEL

Upright post at the head or foot of a stair.

NIGHT FLOWER

Attraction. Drawn to the long ear of a shadow.

NAUTICAL MILE

One sixtieth of a degree of latitude or the length of a minute.

NONPLUSSED

Intrinsic.

NOUVEAU ROMAN

A board used over a window as a valance.

A portion of the wall below a chair.

A salt-box.

A newel.

Eschewing judgment.

Objectivity.

[30]

-O-

THE OCEAN, BETWEEN BUILDINGS

It is a very old road. Its color is original.

The color is not a reflection of the sky.

A thought takes shape inside a wanderer's head.

A page or a letter from her mother's diary.

A paper plane her father had folded.

Keys of nickel to the streets of the city.

OIL MIRACLES

The widow's cruse. Oil in vessels.

Enough bread. A son revived to life.

Flow of the anointing with the Holy Spirit.

ON THE LORD'S DAY, I WAS IN THE SPIRIT

Iron tree in the ocean of grief. *Hallelujah.*

Still and sweet. *Hallelujah.*

Song of the blind woman. *Hallelujah.*

[31]

ONE TIME

That she might have a portion of the blind woman's sable radiant skin, her mantle of anointing, her prayers, the ones moving mountains. *Hallelujah.*

OMOIYARI

Or a form of empathy.

OPEN DOOR

Gold keys are scattered on the piers of the old city. Keep them if you find them on the sidewalks, in the corners. They will open doors for you one day, she says. Lade you with the certainty of sea birds and ships as the blind woman *prays without ceasing* through the night.

ORGANS OF BALANCE

Are most highly developed in the bird.

OTOLITHS

Otoliths press on the ciliae whether the body is at rest or in motion. Otoliths are also stones, *ear stones,* buried in the earth eons ago. *Ear stones,* metaphor of blindness. A mixed metaphor, roughly. Or synaesthesia.

⁓ P ⁓

PALAMPORE

Printed cotton cloth panel from India.

THE PAST TENSES OF GOD'S WORD

Imperishable *I AM.*

PLANTING

My godchild is already in the thumb pots.

When will we see them grow?

They're growing right now.

When will I see them?

PELORUS

A mariner's compass without magnetic needles.

Sight vanes by which bearings are taken.

[33]

PENELOPE

One room, one bed, one tree.

PLACES OF CENTS

Underground, four in a row, on a shelf, under a phone, near pottery, behind the leg of a table, in a store, in the window of a shop, on the windowsill at the library, under the red bristle vine, under the heart, in my pocket, in the soft hands of the blind woman.

PERIPETEIA

A red envelope was flaking silver onto his fingers.
Soon he would become rich at the loss of a loved one.

PIER GLASS

Large mirror between two windows.

POUDREUX

Powdering or dressing table with a disappearing mirror.

PRAYER WITHOUT TRANSLATION

Cuts a quick path through the soul.

PRICE OF WISDOM

Where is it?

How much does it cost?

The deep says, *It is not in me.*

The sea says, *It is not with me.*

PROPERTIES

The wave organ is a sea.

A sense of humor. Her eye, a window.

Vitreous sight to the world.

Comprised of structured spaces, her ear.

The spaces were not in alphabetical order.

They were in approximate alphabetical order.

The tympanum, a drum, the cochlea; malleus, incus, stapes.

A little pressure applied to moments of consciousness.

Accretion of words in her mother's letter, cells of insight.

Q

QUESTIONS ON YELLOW PAPER

The children compose questions on yellow paper and string them together across the room. They have chosen yellow because, they agree, *it is a happy color.* The children look out the window at the rain and the birds flying up. *How does fire burn in the rain? What happened to the birds? Can the ocean burn? Can God be seen? Will the world end? What do the holy scriptures mean by the latter times?*

QUICKSILVER

Is it available at the pharmacy?

They drop quicksilver into the loaves.

When can we see our parents?

A silver vine grows through her heart.

It is an expression of grief.

She is a vine dresser, a vineyard worker.

The rows are marked by certain stones.

Would she be paid the same wages

the other workers earned

at the end of the day?

QUESTION

It seemed odd to her that the word *clover* would appear

instead of *cadaver* in a dream. Clover grows over those

who are resting in the earth, perhaps.

IN *A QUIET LIFE*

Oe said, *The bouquet*

was like a cheerless classmate

with downcast eyes....

-R-

READING

In a quiet corner with downcast eyes.

What are you reading?

Why are you reading?

RECOVERY

Fragrant inside an oiled cabinet.

What happened to the birds?

A widow's cruse.

The son revived to life.

Skies are shorter at the hills.

A paper plane floated over the water.

Its shadow was small as your hand.

I longed to pray the prayer of faith.

A READY SUITCASE

If only you knew, says the blind woman.

This is only me in this hour.

A more slender grace exists inside.

REQUESTS

A bone spur. *Out.*

Miraculous recovery of sight.

An eye she calls her own.

I am well, healed, and whole.

REVEALING DRAMATIC CONSEQUENCES

A land so low, the ocean leans on it.

An oasis of salt mounds.

The patient dedication of scribes.

RIGHT THINGS

She opened her eyes.

The wicks were trimmed.

Oil was readily available.

REAPING

He will send His angels with a great sound of a trumpet, and they will gather together His elect from the four winds, from one end of heaven to the other.

RIPARIAN RIGHTS

A clepsydra.

On the bank of a natural course.

Timed by the fall or flow of water.

The right to use water.

ROSE OF THE WORLD

He exudes an irresistible fragrance.

I am the way, the truth, and the life.

Nine ounces is what a woman's heart weighs.

RUACH

Breath, that most impalpable part of existence, the breath of life.

·S·

SACRAMENTAL

It was the first day.

It's in there, she said. *I can see it.*

The water level inside the iron.

I can see.

She opens a letter in the day room.

SACRIFICE

The price is not greater than God's grace.

AT THE SALT MOUNDS

Children play with scissors.

Cutting boxes and paper for the eclipse.

The desert is entirely salt, blinding salt.

Children are reared amid the salt mounds.

Accustomed to the salt edge of the winds, cutting.

It is not bitterness, they say. It is edifying strength.

SANITY

She whispers *salt.*

SAND-WASHED STREETS

Salt and skin.

SCRIM

Light coarse cotton.

SEA GLASS

Teal, on the other hand, and violet.

To pine is a form of grieving.

I forgot that *pine* is a color.

Certain shades of green.

How long the glass looks broken.

I see my own eye in fragments.

SARGASSUM

Instead of bay leaves and hair money.

[42]

SECOND ROOM

Stone tables. Wings of gold.

Gold box. Gold jar of manna.

A staff that sprouted leaves.

SEDGES AND RUSHES

Grasses have round, hollow stems with solid joints called nodes.

Sedges have solid, three-sided stems with no joints.

Rushes have wiry, round stems and bear their seeds in little pods.

SELF

Lying thalassic in the silence of the unconscious, an ice shelf originates on land and continues out to sea where it rests on the sea bottom. *Self,* I thought. Unseen sheet of ice, heavy trial to the flesh and spirit.

SHADE DIAMETER

A diffusing bowl, essential for study.

An inner bowl (lighting).

[43]

SHELL

A calcareous covering.

An unfinished interior.

A case or covering of a ship.

An arched or domed roof.

A small glass.

A thin layer of stone.

An impersonal manner concealing emotion.

A paper case for holding a charge of powder.

A narrow light racing boat.

A SHUTTER ARRANGEMENT

The blind woman closes the windows.

The way the light enters the room matters.

Too much light sears her vision.

SILL-LENGTH DRAPERIES

Center of attention with a little ingenuity.

SOFTNESS AND DARKNESS

She uses the hard eyebrow pencil instead of the soft one.

She can't see and before she knows it, she's put on far too

much for the soft one. *A wish to see softness and darkness.*

SON OF GOD

I am the rose of the world.

I am the way, the truth, and the life.

Solid mahogany, russeting.

STARBOARD

The right side, looking forward.

SUMMER

She used vinegar, not bleach, to clean a white umbrella.

What is the difference?

One drinks vinegar, not bleach.

One doesn't pickle with bleach.

SAXIFRAGE

I was not strong then as I am now.

Stones had not yet broken under my feet.

Rooted in crevices, time is my strength.

Saxifrage sends it roots deep into stone crevices.

Its name means *stone breaker.*

Living stones bloom in the desert.

·T·

TAIN

A fish eye streaks silver in a tarnished mirror.

THERE IS A BUOY OR A BIRD

There is a buoy or a bird out there, but in the deepest
ocean, where the water is deep enough to be safe for
ships, and where there are no obstructions, there is no
need for buoys.

THALASSIC

... Situated or developed about inland seas.

TINTED

Or a salt-box (silver-gray).

TERATA

... By the sight of miracles.

TOPSIDES

A ship's skin *between water line and rail.*

Is it sweet? asked eyewitnesses.

TWO LIVES

One started over there and one ended here.

One was *an orchid or banyan.*

Or one was a private forest of *a hundred trees.*

One tree bore drops of holy oil.

TWO QUESTIONS

What o'clock is eight bells?

[47]

Time on board a ship is divided into four-hour periods called watches. Eight bells is struck every four hours.

What is a dog watch?

The time between four and eight is divided into two-hour periods called dog watches.

-U-

UPPER ROOM
A flight of stairs, a window in the wall.

UNLEAVENED
There wasn't enough time for the loaves to rise.

- V -

VALUABLES ON THE OCEAN FLOOR

Much of the sea's mineral bounty is invisible.

How can unseen wealth be harvested?

- W -

A WOMAN FACING THE WRONG WAY

Women were arriving at the shore with water and hats and maps. One woman was facing the wrong way, not facing the sea. She was facing the streets and her blue beach hat was reversed. Did she come from a different place?

Perhaps the streets are more interesting than the sea, as the front of the hat is less interesting than the back, where the eyes of indigo plumes rise up, wide open. Has anyone told her? I wondered. One doesn't sit with one's back to the sea. Or perhaps she is simply feeling contrary.

[49]

WARP

Threads running lengthwise in fabric.

WATER GLASS

n. 1: WATER CLOCK 2: a glass vessel (as a drinking glass) for
holding water 3: an instrument consisting of an open box or tube
with a glass bottom used for examining objects in or under water.

WATER MIRACLES

swimming iron

stilling storms

walking on the sea

water into wine

Bethesda Pool

Red Sea

Jordan

Marah

Rephidin

Carmel

WATER OF CONSTITUTION

Water cannot be removed from a certain large molecule without disrupting the entire structure.

Faith cannot be extracted without disrupting life in spirit and flesh. *For other foundation can no man lay than that is laid, which is Jesus Christ.*

WATER TRANSLATION

Each day, she went to the well. As she filled her pail, she listened closely to learn the language. With every drop of water, she picked up a new word. *Ruach* was one. *Breath of life. Terata,* the reactions of eyewitnesses to miracles.

WATERING

The fullness of the Spirit is the condition of His perfect work.

WHAT ASPECTS OF LIFE ARE PAINFUL

Unforgiveness corrupts the soul.
The twisting of a rope like the twisting of a heart.

WHAT ASPECTS OF LIFE ARE SACRED

Life itself.

WATER BEAR

*Tardigrada. Its body shrinks until it looks like a wrinkled seed,
and thus it will remain year after year, to all appearances dead.
If placed in water, however, in a few minutes it will swell out, the
wrinkles will disappear, and gradually it will move. In an hour or
so the creature is as active as ever and crawls away.*

WHY

Tardigrada. Because it's microscopic.

WHAT CURTAINS ARE FOR

To shield the eye from light.

Raw light striking the eye.

She closes the curtains.

When will her eyes be healed?

God is outside time.

It is not a question of when.

[52]

WHAT HAS ALREADY HAPPENED

The oddest of trees, the baobab, is a reservoir of water. Old baobabs are large as houses. A house of water. I would need to learn the language in order to live there. In the dream, however, I had already learned the language and was ready to travel. I had packed my suitcases. *God already is.*

WHAT HASN'T HAPPENED

An innate understanding of faith.

A reservoir of human forgiveness.

Opening a letter.

Her eyes have not bled for another season.

Point of the paper plane seeking the sky.

WRONG THINGS

Refusing to thread a needle.

Refusing to return for the chablis.

Refusing the sharp white wine.

Refusing the offer of grace.

WHAT IS OUT THERE

One calcium atom.

One titanium atom.

A thought. *Yttrium.*

WHAT AND WHAT NOT

Stone chips in water, water in the cologne, a can of bleaching cream, water with a hard edge, a shot of southern comfort, brandy, a hot noon nap. An antique box filled with needles. A brandy decanter, four feet tall, in the day room.

WEDDING

Her hands were unsettled as her notions. Dressing quickly, she put on a hand-stitched wedding veil, flown overseas. She opened her mother's letter. A moth, long asleep, fluttered out. *Life. A piece of paper.* She wondered whether her name was written in the book of life.

WHAT TIMELESSNESS IS

Children float, laughing.

Lightweight houses are built over water.

Glass at the bottom of boats.

Blue tile roofs by request.

The top of the hill is only sea level.

A salt content higher than the inner sea of the body.

The child shows bright salt covering his hands.

Is this *a rare earth metal?* he asks. Will it last forever?

How many rooms should I build in this paper house?

In my Father's house, there are many mansions.

WHAT TO WRITE ABOUT

I found a drop of oil.

I cleaned the table yesterday morning.

Promise me you'll see it.

WHEN PEOPLE ARE LEAVING

Their capacity for hearing becomes immense.

They become living stones.

How many years before I see again?

[55]

WHERE YOU'VE NEVER BEEN

In love.

Indifferent.

Adjoining Asia.

In a composite map of aerial photographs.

WHETHER SAILBOATS FLY

A plane floats. A box of paper floats.

A little salt on the sailboat goes a long way.

This box of breath will wail.

This box of salt will weep.

The blind woman wept blood.

She awaits a miraculous recovery.

WHOM SHE FAILS TO SEE

Ninety pounds in the darkness, mahogany, fragrant,
   weeping.

I am the way, the truth, and the life.

A traitor waited in the shadows, crying out for silver.

[56]

WILLOW

Opened and cleaned by *a spiked drum revolving inside a box.*

WINDOW BOX

For weights counterbalancing a lifting sash.

WIND ROSE

Strength of winds from different directions.

WINDFLOWER

Rue anemone.

WINDOW

Closed by casements or sashes.

A space made for the *admission of light.*

Inside a living stone, this part receives light.

WIND BELL

A bell that is light enough to be moved and sounded by the wind.

WISDOM OF THE EARLY CHURCH

Taking Christ *at His Word.*

WISDOM

Brightness of the firmament.

WOMAN

A literal translation would be *a curved side* or the *closest side* of a man's heart. As she dressed quickly, her heart fluttered like a young finch. *A curved side or the closest side.* A bird whose heart is no larger than a raspberry.

Her father said, the bird looks no larger than a moth. Then how large is a small moth? she asked. No larger than a small clock. It's a mere scrap of paper, he said, as a moth flew across the window, crinkling in the twilight wind.

The young woman quickly readied herself in silence.

A WISE AND UNDERSTANDING HEART

Neither after thee shall any arise like unto thee.

YEARS OF LIFE

wren – 3

thrush – 10

robin – 12

blackbird – 12

goldfinch – 15

partridge – 15

nightingale – 18

peacock – 24

skylark – 30

heron – 60

swan – 100

YELLOW PAPER

A novel written on yellow wallpaper?

Novel Written on Yellow Paper.

The children are writing on yellow paper.

Their questions are strung across the room.

How many pages before this is a book?

How do you write a book?

Must it be written, or can it be told?

Must it tell a story, or can it be a poem?

YES AND *YES*

Where does God live?

Can God live in the pages of a book?

Can you hear God?

Where is God? ask the children.

Yes, says the blind woman, *yes*.

God is before the very beginning.

YONDER

...At or in that distant place usually within sight.

·Z·

ZOE

A man is raised to life. He is breathing slowly, gently,
imperceptibly, a wheel of breath in the body, and then
his eyes are moving right to left, right to left.

Alive in the darkness, a man moves his hands. Over a hun-
dred pounds of spices. Anointed flesh and a sacramental
fragrance of roses. A man is folding up a linen cloth.

We are made in God's image.
The angels have moved the stone.
These words are translated as life.

♦ ♦ ♦

Sources

✦

Book of Knowledge. New York: Pocket Books, 1952.

Bosworth, F. F. *Christ the Healer.* Grand Rapids, MI: Fleming H. Revell, 1973.

Hagin, Oretha. *The Price Is Not Greater than God's Grace.* Tulsa, OK: Faith Library Publications of Kenneth Hagin Ministries, 1991.

Halsey, Elizabeth T. *Ladies' Home Journal Book of Interior Decoration.* Philadelphia: The Curtis Publishing Co., 1954.

The Holy Bible: Old and New Testaments in the King James Version. Giant Print Edition. Nashville: Regency Publishing House, 1973.

[63]

Lewis, Edward V. and Robert O'Brien. *Ships: Life Science Library*. New York: Time Incorporated, 1965.

Lockyer, Herbert. *All the Miracles of the Bible*. Grand Rapids, Michigan: Zondervan, 1961.

Oe, Kenzaburo. *A Quiet Life*. New York: Grove Press, 1990. Translation copyright 1996 by Kunioki Yanagashita and William Wetherall.

Scheffel, Richard L., Ed. *ABC's of Nature*. New York: Reader's Digest Association, 1984.

Webster's Ninth New Collegiate Dictionary. Springfield, Massachusetts: Merriam-Webster, 1985.

Wiersbe, Warren W. *Classic Sermons on the Holy Spirit*. James S. Stewart, "The Wind of the Spirit (1896–1990)." Grand Rapids, MI: Hendrickson Publishers, 1996.

Word of Faith. Broken Arrow, Oklahoma: Hagin Ministries, July 2001.

Notes

♦

Quotation Frontispiece (Bosworth 150)

ACAJOU *Hard tropical wood*... (Halsey 217)

BREAKFRONT *deeper than the sides...china closet.*
(Halsey 217)

BIRTH *The wind bloweth*... (John 3:8)

BACHELOR CHEST *With a folding top*...
(Halsey 217)

BATT *Cotton for filling mattresses*... (Halsey 217)

CARATS (*Book of Knowledge* 243)

CELL *A one-room*... (*such as a word*). (Merriam-
Webster 219)

CHATOYANCY *lined up inside...as the stone is
turned.* (Scheffel 27)

CLICKING SOUNDS *The whispering*...
(Scheffel 184)

CONUNDRUM (Scheffel 26–27)

CASEMENT *on upright hinges* (Halsey 217)

DADO *Part of the wall...* (Halsey 217)

DORMER *A window built into...* (Halsey 217)

DETAIL AT RIGHT *with its one large arm...for a child.* (Halsey 93, 98)

DETAIL AT LEFT *Deep blue is...* (Halsey 131)

DECAY *No sound lasts forever...* (*Book of Knowledge* 50)

ECLOSION *To emerge...* (Merriam-Webster 395)

EIDETIC *Accurate and vivid...* (Merriam-Webster 399)

EAU DE VIE *Water of life... (as pears or raspberries).* (Merriam-Webster 393)

EFFERENT *Outward...* (Merriam-Webster 397)

ELL *Addition...* (Halsey 217)

EMBARCADERO *A landing place...* (Merriam-Webster 405)

EMBER DAYS *A Wednesday...* (Merriam-Webster 405)

EDGE OF FAITH An illustration of faith. (Hagin 23)

EXPLODING THE BOX *Of that day and hour... By your patience...* (Matthew 24:36, Luke 21:19)

ESCRITOIRE *Usually with drawers...* (Halsey 217)

ESCUTCHEON *Ornament used over...* (Halsey 217)

FALSE COVE *In a natural or a false cove...* (Halsey 70)

FIGHTING FISH *A small brilliantly...* (definition for *betta*, Merriam-Webster 146)

A FINE SENSE OF BALANCE *The motion of fluid*... (*Book of Knowledge* 181)

FOG ... *Shuts down*... (*Book of Knowledge* 209)

FUSTIAN *Once a stout cloth*... (Halsey 218)

GRASS FLOWERS *shielded by tough*... (Scheffel 132)

GIRANDOLE *Circular mirror*... (Halsey 218)

THE HEARING OF A FLY *Nearly all insects*... (*Book of Knowledge* 144)

HOW A LIGHTHOUSE IS *Each stone weighs*... (*Book of Knowledge* 209)

HOW NOT TO GRIEVE THE HEART OF JESUS (title is from Bosworth 78)

INNER SPACE *A space*... *One's inner self.* (Merriam-Webster 623)

AN INNING OR AN EAR *Passing through*... *A sympathetic attention.* (definitions for *ear* and *inning*, Merriam-Webster 391–392 & 624)

IN THE MIDST OF THINGS *For as lightning*... *man be.* (Matthew 24:27)

KINDLING POINT *Curved glass*... (*Book of Knowledge* 54 & 45)

KEEL *The backbone*... (Lewis & O'Brien 193)

[67]

A LITTLE WATER EXTENDS LIFE (reference
to Matthew 25:1–13)

LATE FREEZE *a light one...* (Scheffel 107)

LAMBREQUIN *at the top of...* (Halsey 218)

LIVING STONES *Some living stones...until they
flower.* (Scheffel 262)

MACLE *A twin crystal... (as in a mineral).* (Merriam-
Webster 714)

MINERALS *In all, scientists... a living thing.* (Scheffel 26)

MULLION *between panes of glass...* (Halsey 218)

NAMES OF GRASS *orchard...timothy* (Scheffel 132)

NAMES OF WIND *foehn...sirocco* (Scheffel 15)

NEWEL *upright post...of a stair.* (Halsey 218)

NAUTICAL MILE *One sixtieth...length of a minute.*
(Lewis & O'Brien 193)

NOUVEAU ROMAN *A board...salt box.* (Halsey 14
& 217–8)

OIL MIRACLES (Biblical incidents listed in
Lockyer 18)

ON THE LORD'S DAY, I WAS IN THE SPIRIT
(Revelation 1:10)

ORGANS OF BALANCE *Are most highly... (Book
of Knowledge* 181)

[68]

OTOLITHS *Otoliths press on ... ear stones.* (*Book of Knowledge* 181)

PALAMPORE *Printed cotton ... India.* (Halsey 218)

THE PAST TENSES OF GOD'S WORD (Bosworth 127–128)

PELORUS *A mariner's ... bearings are taken.* (Merriam-Webster 868)

PIER GLASS *Large mirror ... windows.* (Halsey 218)

POUDREUX *Powdering ... mirror.* (Halsey 218)

PRICE OF WISDOM *It is not with me.* (Job 28:12)

IN *A QUIET LIFE The bouquet ... eyes.* (Oe 12)

REAPING *He will send His angels ... heaven to the other.* (Matthew 24:31)

RIPARIAN RIGHTS *A clepsydra ... to use water.* (Merriam-Webster 1017)

ROSE OF THE WORLD *I am the way ...* (John 14:6)

RUACH *Breath ...* (Stewart 147)

SACRIFICE *The price ...* (title of Oretha Hagin's *The Price Is Not Greater than God's Grace*)

SCRIM *Light coarse cotton.* (Halsey 218)

SEDGES AND RUSHES Grasses have round ... little pods. (Scheffel 132)

SHADE DIAMETER *A diffusing... (lighting).*
(Halsey 152)

SHELL *A calcareous... light racing boat.* (Merriam-
Webster 1084–1085)

A SHUTTER ARRANGEMENT *The way the
light...* (Halsey 133)

SILL-LENGTH DRAPERIES *Center of attention...*
(Halsey 105)

SON OF GOD *I am the way...* (John 14:6)

STARBOARD *The right side...* (Lewis & O'Brien 193)

THALASSIC *...Situated or...* (Merriam-Webster 1221)

TINTED *Or a salt-box...* (Halsey 14)

TERATA *...By the sight...* (Lockyer 15)

TOPSIDES *between water line...* (Lewis & O'Brien 193)

TWO QUESTIONS *What o'clock... (Book of
Knowledge* 256)

VALUABLES ON THE OCEAN FLOOR *Much
of the sea's...* (Scheffel 49)

WARP *Threads running lengthwise...* (Halsey 219)

WATER GLASS *n. 1: WATER CLOCK...* (Merriam-
Webster 1332)

WATER MIRACLES *swimming iron... Carmel*
(Lockyer 18)

WATER OF CONSTITUTION *Water cannot...*

For other foundation... (Merriam-Webster 1332,

1 Corinthians 3:11)

WATERING *The fullness of the Spirit...*

(Bosworth 158)

WATER BEAR *Tardigrada...crawls away.* (*Book of*

Knowledge 132)

WHAT CURTAINS ARE FOR *Raw light...*

(Halsey 145)

WHAT HAS ALREADY HAPPENED *The oddest*

of... (Scheffel 108–109)

WHAT IS OUT THERE *One calcium atom...* (*Book*

of Knowledge 39)

WHAT TIMELESSNESS IS *In my Father's...*

(John 14:2)

WILLOW *a spiked drum...* (Merriam-Webster 1350)

WINDOW BOX *For weights counterbalancing...*

(Merriam-Webster 1351)

WIND ROSE *Strength of winds...* (Merriam-Webster

1351)

WINDFLOWER *Rue anemone...* (Merriam-Webster

1351)

WINDOW *Closed by casements...* (Merriam-Webster 1351)

WIND BELL *A bell that is light enough*... (Merriam-Webster 1351)

WISDOM OF THE EARLY CHURCH *at His Word.* (Bosworth 52)

WISDOM *Brightness of the*... (Daniel 12:3)

A WISE AND UNDERSTANDING HEART *Neither after*... (1 Kings 3:12)

YEARS OF LIFE *wren*... *100* (*Book of Knowledge* 130)

YELLOW PAPER (references to works by Charlotte Perkins Gilman and Stevie Smith, "The Yellow Wallpaper" and *Novel Written on Yellow Paper)*

YONDER *...At or in that*... (Merriam-Webster 1369)

ZOE *These words*... (Bosworth 149)

The Author

♦

Karen An-hwei Lee lives and teaches on the West Coast. Her chapbook of prose poems, *God's One Hundred Promises*, received the Swan Scythe Press Prize. A regular contributor to literary journals, she has completed several novellas and poetry collections. Her work has won numerous university awards, fellowships, and residencies, including a fellowship from the Yoshiko Uchida Foundation. She holds an M.F.A. in creative writing and a Ph.D. in literature.

Tracy Estelle Tipton

[73]